For my family

First published 2021 by Macmillan Children's Books
an imprint of Pan Macmillan
The Smithson, 6 Briset Street, London EC1M 5NR
EU representative: Macmillan Publishers Ireland Limited,
Mallard Lodge, Lansdowne Village, Dublin 4
Associated companies throughout the world
www.panmacmillan.com

Hardback ISBN: 978-1-5290-1358-0
Paperback ISBN: 978-1-5290-1359-7

1 3 5 7 9 8 6 4 2

A CIP catalogue record for this book is available from the British Library.

Printed in China

MIX
Paper from responsible sources
FSC® C116313
FSC www.fsc.org

↑ Open this way

Penguin Parcel

Victoria Cassanell

MACMILLAN CHILDREN'S BOOKS

Polar Bear lived a quiet life,
and that was just the way he liked it.

Until one day something in the newspaper caught his eye.

Hmmm . . . thought Bear, *it could be fun to have a pet.*

A penguin would be nice.

He waited in all day for his delivery . . .

. . . but it still got left on the doorstep.

Polar Bear was so happy with his new pet.

He looked just like the picture in the paper.

Polar Bear stroked
Penguin,

brushed him,

snuggled with him

and took him for walks.

They went swimming

and did some drawing.

Polar Bear told Penguin how he loved to knit.

They went sledging

and built snow creatures.

Having a pet penguin was really lovely, until . . .

Polar Bear noticed there was something wrong with Penguin.

He wouldn't sleep in his bed,

he wouldn't eat his pet food,

and he wouldn't cuddle anymore.

Polar Bear tried his best to cheer up Penguin.
But Penguin didn't seem to like whale watching.

He wasn't impressed by the northern lights, either.

Then one day, things went from bad to worse . . .

Penguin went missing!

Polar Bear searched high and low, far and wide . . .

. . . but there was no sign of Penguin

and it was getting later and later.

At last, Polar Bear found him.

Polar Bear was beginning to understand what the problem could be . . .

. . . and how he could fix it.

The next day, they set off,

through forests,

over deserts

and across oceans.

They travelled a long, long way, from the top of the world to the bottom, until they finally spotted something in the distance.

Penguin and Polar Bear said their goodbyes,

then Penguin ran to join his family.

Seeing that Penguin was happy again,
Polar Bear headed home.

Penguin was overjoyed to be back where he belonged.

And, even though they were far, far away from each other . . .

. . . Polar Bear and Penguin always kept in touch.